THE
SMALL
DOOR OF
YOUR
DEATH

THE SMALL DOOR OF YOUR DEATH

POEMS

Sheryl
St. Germain

Autumn House Press

Pittsburgh

pennsylvania
COUNCIL ON THE ARTS

This project was supported by the Pennsylvania Council on the Arts, a state agency, through its regional arts funding partnership, Pennsylvania Partners in the Arts (PPA). State government funding comes through an annual appropriation by Pennsylvania's General Assembly. PPA is administered in Allegheny County by Greater Pittsburgh Arts Council.

Cover art: "Gray" by Morgan Everhart. Oil on canvas. 72 x 96 inches. 2015.
Cover design: Kinsley Stocum

ISBN: 978-1-938769-27-6

Library of Congress Control Number: 2017951940

TABLE OF CONTENTS

1.

2.

3.

4.

5.

I tried to kill the pain, bought some wine
And hopped a train
Seemed easier than just a waitin' around to die

—Townes Van Zandt, "Waiting Around to Die"

1.

Loving an Addict

yesterday the skies were troubled
gusts almost knocked us down

today sun, the kiss of a breeze

it was always fights or lies

maybe at the end

       I preferred the lies

Son Poem

he'll have thin and careless hair,
strong and directionless, indifferent

to brushes, a wisp of tail
that suckles his back like a vine

some nights you'll look at him
and see your death

and once or twice, in the second
that you blink

you'll see yourself, grinning
and beckoning with unwashed hands

Louisiana Oranges

Huge as softballs, sweet as honey,
the rind so intensely orange that
the smell lingers on your hands long after eating it.

My grandmother married under an orange tree.
She wore a tiara of orange blossoms in her hair.

This one cost fifty cents in the French market,
and before I leave I'll draw in all its sweetness,
let it run down my mouth.

The market is full of color and breath,
the sun, a great orange lighting the sky,
and I've not had a drink for three months.

The Good Mother

My son's small, maybe six, has just bathed and brushed his teeth. Toys scattered on the floor, a box of LEGOs here, some half-built castles there, Ninja Turtles stacked like a pile of corpses in the corner, pants peeled off and left in the middle of the room, stuffed animals heaped on his bed.

He's under the covers, hair still damp, cheeks shining. He smells like any child just out of a bath, fragile and wild, pure as the finest milled soap. I grab a book, tuck him in, and start to read.

I'm sober, done with drugs. All that's alive and good is in this room: my voice, his eyes, large and trusting, waiting for the story.

Suit of Swords

This, the family into which we were born,
all edges and blades, a seeing so sharp
some of us are driven to blunt
all the ways we hurt.

My son, the little sword, is trying to sleep,
but he's tossing and turning, cutting himself
and me when I try to help.

Another difficult day. Nothing
is as either of us had hoped.
Missing homework, notes about
disobedience written in angry
scrawls. He *doesn't pay attention,*
doesn't play well with others.
The principal has taken
to paddling him. Teachers and shrinks
peddle pills to settle us both.
Every day I wake up, he says,
and promise myself I'll be good.
I really want to but—something always happens.

He falls into a fit of sobs, choking.
I stroke him to sleep, singing some song
about summertime. I know only too well
that will is not enough for change,

but I'm a sword too,
and have little else to offer.

Christmas, 2013

He's no longer a boy, but a young man
with eyes that ask to be left alone.

I'm driving him to his apartment
after two days of cooking, movies, holiday cheer.

I don't know, Mom, he says suddenly,
through tears, *what will become of me.*

I freeze and thaw, unsure of what to do—
always that dance of how much touching
he wants, how much I can stand to give.

Three of Swords

All bad news creeps through phones, voices cracking and flat
over the years and miles: *it burned down*, son says of the garage,
he's dead, mother says of brother, *dead*, sister says of nephew,
house flooded, other sister says,
dead, mother says of aunt, *dead* brother,
dead father, drunk, heart attack, overdose,
totaled your car,
I'm leaving, says the son.

The Rhetoric of Wrecks

Wrecks sing softer in winter—
      swells of snow on roadsides
            cradle cars that lost their fight with ice.
    Snow muffles the crash, the shouts,

the wrestling with doors and belts, the retching. Even blood
and breath disappear in blizzards.

We slide and pirouette on black ice,
      wrapping cars around other cars,
           circling to face the end head on. The last
                sound we hear is percussion, requiem,
                    the sacred music of metal against metal.

                      If we've had enough to drink,
                we may be lucky not to hear the song
                    of our own dying:
                    oh silent night, oh holy night.

Nine of Swords

every nightmare a dream
of someone we love

A Perfect Game

—after Robert Hayden

Sundays too, I tell my son, your grandfather drank—
at the bowling alley between strikes and spares and claps on the back.

I loved to watch him make the approach for his shot:
how serious, how attentive to his posture,

the placement of his hands, his eyes never
wavering from the pins, the ball sent on its sure arc,

hooking into the headpin at just the right angle
for all to fall down. Often, in the early years,

he would bowl a perfect game, twelve strikes
in a row, no matter how much he drank. Somehow

drink and skill merged for a time into the poetry
of a flawless act. Sometimes we would drive with him

to tournaments far away, fear gripping us as he woozed
back home, barely avoiding the crashes he would have

in the future. Time passed, he bowled fewer strikes,
and his trophies migrated to the hall closet,

piled up one on the other, so many forgotten
bodies: bronze statues of the same faceless man

with the golden ball, his name plated at the bottom.
Before he died he met me for dinner

one last time, hands trembling,
voice quaking, almost incoherent. He couldn't eat,

would only drink cup after cup of black coffee.
I was still a child. What did I know,

what did I know, of a father's Stygian alleys,
of drink's guttered offices?

Minus Ten Degrees

The cold, bolder than any drug,
holds you close. Your heart
slows, body turns brittle—

The sound of a phone ringing
in the night might break you
in half.

Knight of Swords

You call in the middle of the night
to tell me you'll never stop drinking
because *it feels so good.*

You aren't like your grandfather and uncle,
you say, long dead of it,
you are you,
and you'll go out your own way.

Maybe, you slur, *I'll do it now.*

At a Writer's Retreat in France, Not Drinking

He calls long distance to tell me
he's stopped drinking, and will I help him,
tell him about my own journey.
Yes, I say, *yes*, almost giddy with joy.
He can't stay on the phone, but he promises
to call, he's sorry, he says, for not calling
more often. I hang up, holding my breath.

What, I think, can I say to him?

Every night here, I could tell him,
the writers stay up late drinking, talking,
tasting the wines, discussing their merits or shortcomings.
Sometimes they drink the special local champagne,
sometimes a neighbor invites us for aperitifs
or the owner of this place brings out
his homemade cherry wine or dandelion wine
or elderberry wine, and I think they would even make
chocolate wine here if they could.

I've said *no thanks* every night for two weeks,
for two weeks gone to bed early
with my fragile sobriety.

When I wake to look at the mountain
outside my window, it seems the world is nothing
but vineyards. Should I tell him
how sorry I am not to bond with others
in that way one can over drinks,
when everyone is relaxed and loose-tongued,

how sorry to hold myself apart?
Should I tell him I don't miss
the drinking itself: of that
I have memories for a lifetime.

Sober, I'd say, I'm quieter, a little more awkward.
More interesting to myself, I'm certain
I bore others. *Oh*, my new French friends say,
you could just have a sip, a glass, a taste,
couldn't you, but they don't know
the One who will not stop
with any sip or taste.

Should I tell him the air here
smells like grapes and lavender,
should I describe how it feels
when I close my eyes,

something wild, ever present,
stilled
for the moment.

Letter to My Son, Winter

Come home. There's so much I want to tell you. Today, two years sober, eyes burning with a white as cold and unforgiving as an unwritten poem, I walk into the backyard. Snow, snow, and more snow. White, white, more white.

Wait. Look harder. The brown bones of the swamp rose to the south reach out of snow and then fall back, clean, pure and budless. Stalks of coneflowers are stripped of petal and color but dark seedpods hold on like iron. It's the way I find myself holding onto days without you as they stay white and cold and do not change.

Come home. It's not boring, I promise. Thistle and black sunflower seeds pepper the ground under the feeder, a small piece of chaos in all this sobriety. The birdbath's filled with frozen water, snow on top like icing on a cake you cannot eat.

Come home. The cottontail that ate our lettuce—remember?— sleeps, curled near the back of the house. I see a feather, dark blue against white. I see tracks of squirrel and rabbit and dog, silver-blue and blazing on the ground where they've melted and refrozen. I see the weakness of the structure of our house—how all the snow falls off the steep roof to one part where much of it turns to ice and swells the gutters, melts and refreezes on the back porch. I'm sure the gutters will soon fall from the weight.

All this I see because of snow and its dark sister: a kind of brutal cold that stings you awake when you walk out into it, a cold you can almost see, the way you can see the water someone splashes on your face to wake you from a drunken reverie.

In that moment, you remember everything.

[*I sleep*]

I sleep for what seems like days, have fever dreams filled with confusing letters that don't resolve into words, hallways with no end, vampires whose eyes are Os, whose teeth are versions of the letter V. Dreams where I can't speak.

I wake, feeling scraped and gutted. I can't even remember what I call myself anymore. I stumble out into the street, steal a lady's purse after she exits a pharmacy, swallow some pills from a bottle I find inside. I see an image of myself in a store window, pale, all edges, my eyes like jagged cuts in my face.

I get picked up for vagrancy and spend the night in jail. I try to write on the walls of the cell. I can't read my own handwriting.

Ten of Swords

You're in an airport somewhere
waiting for a plane when he calls,
his voice heavy and dark, his words
like sludge.
         He says
he's checking himself into rehab.

He hadn't slept, he says, for three days.
Too much meth and heroin,
I thought I'd become a vampire,
he says, *I attacked my friend, tried to kill him.*

His voice, a shock wave, enters you.
Meth, heroin. Your chest burning, heavy.
What, not even an *en garde*?

I kept throwing up blood, he says. *I thought*
it was your blood.

            Later, on the plane,
you imagine what it must have looked like,
the friend's bedroom, his shirt soaked in blood,
him thinking he's murdered you.
                You see him
rushing at the friend, fists purpled with rage,
you see the girlfriend trying to calm him,
you see him pushing her away, her head

hitting the wall. You see him, you see him.

I felt a death rattle,
he said.

Touché.

Feral

Four months before you die,
you show up at my door
skittish, sober, not yourself,
whatever that self is,
like a dog lost too long in the woods

    all you once hoped to be
    still lights your face, though:
    it is almost a holy light

you are trying to be a good man
you are trying to live in this world
that you hate

    I love that you still care enough
    to pretend to be
    the one I named,
    hoped to birth.

2.

Rehab

we're here, our skin thin as parchment
eyes ringed with grief
hearts swollen and scarred

to visit on prescribed days, to come
together with you and your wounded
brothers

it's hard to hope, but we cling
to any worm of it

                          the lights
in the rooms here, after all, are so bright

Crook

We're sure the silence
means you're using again.
*I could just as easily
go back to being a crook*, you'd said,
I'm too young to be sober for the rest of my life,

as if sobriety was a weight too heavy to bear.
The word that haunts, though, is *crook*,
the old-fashionedness of it, for one—

could you not stand to use the word *thief*,
or *criminal?* We don't know all the ways of
your crookedness, and are left to imagine

what you might be doing to stay alive
and high. C*ulprit, wrong-doer, shyster, cheat,
swindler, burglar, scam artist, felon,*

con-man—from Old Norse *krokr: hook, corner.*
Too crook to work, the Australians say,
meaning *sick*, and here, in street slang *that shit be crook,*

meaning *totally awesome*, meaning you, our son,
our brother, our friend,
that one high as a kite, that one lit,

cranked, amped, baked, stoned, fried,
toasted, that one stealing money
from a girlfriend, pain pills
from a grandmother, that one
erasing the path as he goes.

Seven of Swords

the man's creel is filled with fish
but he keeps fishing

it's the season

he will take
everything he can get

Great Midwest Flood, 1993

> —*We admitted we were powerless over alcohol, that our lives had become unmanageable.* The Big Book

Nothing I did could have stopped
the heavy snowfall the winter before,
or the deep rains of spring and summer,
nothing could have stopped the swelling
of the Mississippi, the Missouri, the Des Moines,
Illinois, Iowa, Skunk, or Raccoon. Not

my fault, the way the flood knocked
our house from its moorings,
the way the water got so high
you couldn't tell a town had been there,
nothing I could do about the water supply
getting contaminated, or all the bridges
that were knocked out, the river traffic
halted, I couldn't stop

the houses and bodies from floating down the river,
or the levees from breaking, or the waters
from crashing into towns, not my fault,
the state declared a disaster area.

I try to remember how powerless I was
then, as the drunks in my family line up now,
the rivers rising, so many bodies
it seems all I can do is sit on the bank and watch,
the floodwaters lapping sweetly at my feet,
my father and brothers calling out,

jump in, the water's fine.

Ode to Needles

I'm trying hard to recognize the different trees
on this stranger coast: spruces, firs, pines,
but it comes down to needles, really,
their color and shape, how they're bundled,
even how they smell:
blue spruce needles are blue green,
sometimes silver, sharp pointed at the tip,
four sided. When crushed they smell
intoxicating, like a rich piney wine.

White spruce's are also blue green,
but with bone-colored lines.
They're sharp pointed, too,
but when crushed smell shitty, like skunk.

Douglas fir's are dark yellow or blue green,
flat and flexible with rounded tips.
Western white and sugar pine come in bundles of five,
lodgepole pine in bundles of two, the needles
stout, sometimes twisted.

I look at the trees over and over, touching and smelling,
trying to memorize their shapes and colors,
trying to forget, for a moment, the needles
I know best, the ones I used in my youth,
the ones you'll use in yours.

They come in bundles of six. Silver and round
except at the ends, which are flatter and sharp pointed,
they're always attached to the end of a plastic 1 mL syringe.

Never twisted, they're hard to crush. They smell
like hospitals, and when I enter my vein
with one, I think of spruce
and fir and pine. I'm injecting a resinous sap,
the shot is a prayer.

Lotus-Eaters

You had no Odysseus to order you back to the ship,
command that you stop, but sometimes it's hard to believe

you didn't at least have one first choice, like those lotus-eaters of old,
wolfing flowers that made them forget home.

Some days you must have woken horrified you were still
on the island, grieving the wasted years, wanting change.

But you'd lived so long in that foreign land
it must have felt more home than home.

I remember only too well the taste of that sweetness.

Ace of Swords

I'm good
at stealing little things.

I wish I could brag
to my mother.

I keep getting drunk.
It makes me feel like music.

Eight of Swords

A woman is walking through a destroyed landscape, a forest of pines and swords. The swords are words, the words she doesn't have, words she can't say.

She would like to speak, but when she does, swords come out instead of words.

After Dinner, He Walks Outside and I Imagine What He's Thinking

It's winter. Snowing big fat flakes. He looks up to feel them on his face. He's cold everywhere. Even his heart feels cold. He doesn't think anyone can understand how cold a heart can get. *Fuck this shit*, he thinks. He looks around. People walking everywhere in paths through snow. They look as if they have something to do, somewhere to go. He stumbles past a church.

The snow comes down heavier, and he wonders what it would be like to float, alone, a single thing of beauty singing its way to earth. Maybe that's what a soul is like, he thinks.

The flakes fall, soften, disappear into his cheeks. He wonders if it's too late.

Facebook Post: Three Weeks Before He Dies

—a found poem

Sometimes I get way too excited. Mostly
I try to battle my natural TMI tendencies,
which often results in my seeming standoffish

or simply weird to others. I honestly don't have
a natural social mode. Sometimes I succumb

to clinical depression and stop talking to everyone
for months or years. Most prominently, I feel
super awkward. I have stopped trying to fix this.

There are things that will not change.
And I think that ultimately most people that matter
find me likeable. Which is nice. Things break down
from time to time but there are constants:
People who stick around. Family. Good friends
that will pick up the phone even if it's been a couple years.

I'm lucky. I'm really lucky. Might even say blessed.
This is 30, and I think I'm ready to cool it
on the white whine a bit and just give thanks.

Oh yeah . . . it's thanksgiving wtf. haha.
So thanks y'all. You know who you are.

Eight of Swords

She keeps putting the card back in the deck and shuffling.

She wants another card, a card filled with hope, a card that's not Swords, a card that is Cups, maybe, Wands, a card that has a round woman eating and drinking and laughing.

But every time she picks again, it's the eight of swords, the woman blindfolded, caged by swords as tall as she is, their points buried in the ground.

Her husband says it's just chance, it doesn't mean anything.

[*it comes down to this*]

it comes down to this:

a friend's bedroom, a needle, you
newly clean,

a small envelope of dope
that delivers the same dose

as always, though this time
it's been so long, your body's forgotten

what to do
with so much

~

you choose the vein
in the back of a hand
to carry

this last intimacy
a puncture mark

     the small door

of your death

~

did you feel it, in those last seconds,
that sudden rush
    of sun, warmth,

    of all you thought
        you wanted?

~

you slip into sleep so deep
the body forgets to breathe

you feel nothing,
not the cold water

of those trying to baptize you back,
or the thin lips of the friend
breathing into you,

not the pounding on your heart,
the percussion that breaks two of your ribs

or the paramedics giving up,
signing *time*
of death

Two of Swords

Night. The heavens
brilliantly bruised—
purple, black, violet.

Someone's face pounded open,
beaten like a piece of meat
spread out as sky.

3.

Benediction: A Suite

We named you *Gray* because we hoped for you the thousands of hues that sing between black and white. A world of nuance. An Adams' photo of cloud and rock and sky, filled with uncountable shadows, a life lived in twilight, in fantastical stories we would read together, stories peopled with elves and wizards and mountains. A name for one we hoped would follow his own path, wild as wolf or heron or whale, though we knew, too, that gray's the color of mourning, ambiguity.

After you die, I grieve by stitching a blanket of the most sumptuous yarns, each a slightly different shade of gray: blue-gray, pearl-gray, reddish-gray, silver-gray, a gray that's almost black. Every few rows a shock of white—popcorn stitches. They light up the blanket like small lamps, round and full of hope. I surround the white stitches with coal black, fringe the ends so the blanket dances.

I feel you in my fingers as I go: angry, loving. With each round my hands remember your sadness and wildness, with each row a wish I could have stitched your wounds as confidently as I do this blanket.

This is my way, not yours, but oh how I wish you'd found a different kind of needle, a hook, some balls of breathtaking yarn, a place to sit in for a time and let it all wash over you.

I understand wanting freedom from pain, even if it comes from a bottle or syringe. I know what it's like to white-knuckle yourself to sobriety, to wrench yourself from what you've become and wait, miserable for a time, until you take root in another soil, but I couldn't force you to walk to a safer place.

Instead, too late, these words of slate and silver, gunmetal, ash, charcoal, red ochre and quartz, grays dark as storm clouds, warm as your eyes when you used to smile, bone-light as your ashes.

4.

Viewing the Body

If some spirit of you remains, something not caught in the corporeal, it will surely not sport the dark beard you were so proud of, or your smell of soap and smoke. It will not have your hair, nut-brown and flowing like a river, this hair I stroke now, tentatively, as if it would disturb if I touched too deeply. It will not have your laugh, your eyes shimmering with questions and wounds.

Invulnerable in death, perhaps you'll become some terrifying angel. Or will you evaporate into millions of breaths flowing through sky and water and earth?

Whatever.

Never again this body, never this vessel through which I knew you.

[*there were signs everywhere*]

there were signs everywhere:

danger
steep curve
deadly currents
no swimming

end of the road

oh but

for some of us life's a garment
that's never fit right, made of a fiber
to which we're allergic.

skin not enough to protect you,
physician's pills like candy

Overdose: What They Say to Comfort Mothers

a disease
        think *cancer, diabetes*

        genetic
                think *father, brothers*

                hardwired
                        think *chemistry, dopamine*

        x = x
                nothing you could do

        fate

                        ~

they show photographs
        of the brain on drugs, off drugs, on, off, on, off,

highlight with colored light the areas
        damaged by drugs
they cite identical twin studies
        conduct genetic experiments with mice

tell you the A1 allele of the dopamine receptor D2
        is more common in people addicted to alcohol or cocaine

                        ~

their numbers, charts, and figures,
their medical words, hopeless

blaze away, hopeless
at the startled soul

In a Church Two Weeks After Your Death

Christmas, it's all lights and wreaths,
a life-size crèche with a statue of the baby Jesus.
Above, a statue of Mary holding the infant in her arms.

I don't believe, but here I am lighting a candle.

She lost a son too, I suddenly remember,
could do nothing

                    for his suffering.

The Drop

We meet in the parking lot of a church
as if it's some kind of drug deal. He gives me
half of what's left of you.

A velvet maroon sack with a gold tie,
a black plastic box inside.

I notice again how his hands and yours are so alike,
your plump lips, your sweetly crooked smiles.

We've been divorced most of your life,
and he murmurs something about
this being *the last Gray switch*.

He's right. I take the sack with my half of you
and walk away.

We Call Them Ashes

But they're nothing like ashes, which are flimsy and light,
ready to disappear into the slightest wind.

What they really are: ground bones from your skeleton,
all that was unburnable in the hell of the crematorium,

heavy with substance, gravel-like, each particle distinct,
the color of shells bleached by sun.

~

I sit on a high rock where you'd sit as a child,
looking out over a creek where you swam,
where you caught your first fish, a small bass. I dig my hands
into the bits of bone and grit. Greedy for touch,
they gather under my fingernails.

I'm terrified of this intimacy
death has brought us.

Your dust covers my feet and legs on its way down.
I dip again and again until almost nothing remains.
Gravity takes what's left of you to join water, rock, and bone

I watch what's left swirl in the eddies of the creek.

The Grief Committee

One is some sort of cleaning woman
constantly sweeping and dusting,
straightening chairs, moving the furniture
around. A pile of what she calls
rubbish lurks in one corner of my heart.
Her vote is to wipe our hands of it all,
empty out every spidery space,
get on with it, throw it all out.

Another sits in a farther corner at a small desk
doing mathematical proofs and equations
over and over, *if this, then that*, she scribbles,
x plus y equals n, heroin plus benzos equals death,
meth plus alcohol plus asthma equals death,
if only *x* had not happened, if only *y*,
this plus *this* still equals *this*, *this* subtracted
from *this* still equals *this*, *this* divided by *this*
still equals *this*. It is still a mystery; she must
start all over again.

In another corner skulks a crazy woman,
hair unbrushed and matted,
dark circles rimming her eyes. Fingernails
bit to blood, she's mad with sorrow.
She will have nothing to do with the cleaning
of houses or the doing of sums.

First Snow

Tenuous and hesitant
it falls
     so wet it's hardly snow

         see, you can make it
into a weapon: gather
            its moisture tight
            into the core
of your palm, kernel
          your fingers into a fist

The Drug-Pusher Friend Speaks

His mother called me the day after he died in my house.
She was crying, shouting, saying I'd killed her son,

that I'd sold him drugs, that I might as well
have stuck the needle in him myself.

She said she hoped I'd die.

She said someone should kill me.

I said he got the stuff from some homeless person.

I said I was an addict.

I said he was an addict.

I said he was my friend.

Less a Song Than a Compilation of Beats

                                                            to start here,
                                                            on this side,

                                              because you were never
                                                                    where
                                                        everyone else lived

never where
everyone else began
never where
we wanted you to be:

safe, anchored
in normalcy

tolerant of boredom,
the tedium of the daily

                              ~

you were pulled into the world,
whole and full-throated

                                                        but in that place
                                                      you never let us enter

                                                    the years would nurture
                                                                  a crack

                                                        it was always there
                                              underneath your lopsided smile,
                              underneath the laugh everyone called infectious,
                                              maybe because it was so rare,

that when it came
it seemed to explode
out of you
and for that minute,
we all felt happy

the crack:
the way you folded your arms
high across your chest,
as if protecting your heart
from some predator
we couldn't see

I've come to think you heard a music
melancholy, mellifluous,
some seductive tune
we couldn't hear

a soundtrack
to which you fit your actions

until no one could ignore
the pulsing beats
that never quite
seemed to morph into song

we were always too late,
coming on the scene just after
you'd drank so much
you'd vomited blood

or swallowed or smoked
or snorted or pumped into your veins
universes of drugs
and had become nothing

but fists and curses

we consulted doctors, therapists,
books friends-who-had-sons-
like-ours said to read

but we felt helpless
trying to inject love and logic
like it was Naloxone

                                        In rehab you introduced yourself
                                              as *addict, alcoholic*
                                                 for the first time

                                                      you talked
                                         about spending rent money
                                   on drugs, about drinking every day
                                       for ten years, you said you were
                                       a *trash-can addict*, you did it all,
                                     meth, heroin, pills, if it was called
                                              dope you had done it

we made lists of what we thought
was wrong, a mixtape of symptoms
and needs we played over and over
in our heads, riffing off one, then another
'til we knew them by heart

still when I looked at you
it was *Gray*, I saw, not an addict,
but a troubled son

we sewed you together during the day,

                                                                you unraveled by dusk

frenzied and free,
each night you worked that song
you'd never finish

5.

Canal in Amsterdam

Swans nestle tiny chicks
under a diamond sky:

your absence

Windmills

indifferent, split the air
we cannot see what they power

grief moves through the body
touching every part of you

Four of Swords

We should take care, Einstein said,
not to make the intellect our god,
and this is why the woman lies

on the stone floors of the church
staring at the stained-glass windows

she is trying to conjure up a god
she could believe in, but when she
closes her eyes all she feels is the edge

of her spine, resting for now,
as much as swords can rest

Black Mountain, France

Sometimes you're shocked at how
a land has bared itself to you

walking a mountain road,

you stop, electric
suddenly aware

the trees whisper
excruciating intimacies

a blood memory
from before you were born

Summer Solstice, 2015

You've been dead six months and twelve days. I draw back the curtains and open the window as far as it will open to breathe in the morning air. The sun's rising over the treed mountains as far as you can see. Enthusiastic birds sing as if their lives depended on getting the song just right, insects buzz as if already drunk on the day, roosters crow. It's morning in rural France, the longest day of the year.

You would hate it.

I head out for my daily walk, choosing a winding path where I'll have to brush by rosemary bushes as big as small cars, and budding lavender. I tread on wild mint, spot tiny wild strawberries and foxglove, roses and grape vines. The air is redolent with the wild perfume of morning.

You were always a person of night, even as a child, before the drinking, the pills, and all the rest. When you grew to be a man, it got worse; it was almost as if you were allergic to sunlight. Some days you never saw sun at all.

This day, the longest of the year, you would understand as the shortest night. I stay up until the sun goes down, watching outside the window as the sky darkens.

Today, I'll walk another day without you.
I'll carry you in me, like before you were born,
on these walks.

It's night everywhere in me,
so it should feel like home.

Old Fish

This is what she knows:
whether water is sweet or salt or poison,
that shadows and ripples signify death,
that nets are invisible in water.

In times of drought I've found her
half dead, having scooped out a womb
of damp earth with her armless body.
She covers herself with wet sand,

and still lives, her skin
having secreted something
to keep her alive until the next rain.

On a Trail in the Languedoc

—in memory, Tiny Mulder

If I must leave this world, let it be now,
in midsummer, when the sun is nothing

more than itself in the brave sky,
its job to light and nourish never

clearer, let it be in a valley such as this,
treed mountains hugging either side,

showing the way. Let the brook beside me
be noisy and blessed with trout I will never catch,

let it blather and blab, giving away nothing
of its secrets, let there be abundant

fig trees, heavy with fruit I will never
pick, let wildflowers be bragging

and ecstatic everywhere I look,
and let some of them have names I do not

know. Let there be a cool breeze
and, oh, let there be butterflies

of rich and many colors I have never seen,
and fat bees gathering honey I will never

taste, let me be content that
my legs are still able

to carry me down this trail,
so clearly lit by sun.

Versions of Heaven

1.

It's the early nineties, we're dancing alone in the house
to a mixtape I made of R.E.M., you're small and we're wild

with music, which I've turned up: *Calling on, in transit,*
calling on, in transit, radio free Europe, radio free Europe,
you're laughing and turning round and round, we take
a breather, then another one starts: *And the train conductor says*
Take a break Driver 8, Driver 8 take a break,

we're pumped, twisting and high with adrenaline,
and I've had a couple glasses of wine.
I kiss your cheek and say *one more before bath time.*
Drums, jangly guitars, you can almost imagine them
singing in some garage:
please find my harborcoat, can't go outside without-ou-ou-out it,
we try to sing along, but those are the only words we understand,
we're clowns,
laughing, swinging, bowing, twisting until we're out
of breath, *my harborcoat, can't go outside without it,*
we don't even know what a harborcoat is, but we want one—

breathing hard, I scoop you up,
maybe it's in the bathtub,
I say as you flail, joy,
in my arms.

2.

A summer day, we're driving somewhere in Iowa,
through monolithic cornfields and the rare small prairie.

The sun makes us feel happy after a long winter.
I point out flowers on the side of the road, compass plants, coneflowers.

You're putting song after song in the CD player for me,

calling out the coolness of this one, the craft of that:
listen to this, Mom, and this, and this—

I don't know how we're still in our bodies.

3.

We're driving again, unable to speak
because of some recent argument.
                    You put in Uncle Tupelo,
skip to something without lyrics, "Sandusky,"
turning it up as loud as it will go.
          That high-tuned guitar melody,
            melancholy and insistent,
            something hard that needs to be said,
                      the clucking banjos fighting to keep it light.

I don't know if you know how much I love this song,
how much it means to speak like this.

4.

I'm sitting at home alone
in front of the computer.
I haven't seen you in a year.

You've sent me a music video of your band.
Your hair's shorter, a beard.
A keytar's swung around your shoulder,
the hint of a smile on your face,

your mind aches and your body shakes . . .

I play the video again and again, just for the smile.

5.

I'm sitting in the back of an Austin club watching you
deejay into the early morning hours,

        hands and fingers spidering between turntables and computers,
    monster headphones cupping your ears,

pushing buttons

      as if your life were there

it's not music I care for, all electronic loops
without end or meaning.
If I weren't trying so hard to like it,
I'd say it was drug music.

You're probably loaded, but you seem happy.
The audience likes what you're doing,
and I drink you in like a wine I can never
get enough of. We could stay here
forever, or long as the high lasts.

6.

We're dancing at my wedding to the song you picked for the mix:
> *It's no problem of mine but it's a problem I find*
> *living a life that I can't leave behind. . .*

You give your crooked smile,
> twirl around as you did when you were a boy.

7.

I don't believe in it, really,
      golden gates, singing choirs of angels, the whole bit,
          but I like to imagine a place where you might be
          with the denizens of my childhood faith,

      playing songs for saints,
         sampling the sounds of angels' trumpets,
      mixing hip-hop versions of Gregorian chants,

recording the chill sounds of wings fluttering,
         showing the gone ones how to shuffle saint's voices,
how to scat god's breath.

The Truth Is

heaven and hell
are the same place for an addict.

But what, anyway, has truth ever had to do
with heaven.

Reasons to Live: The Color Red

cowboy boots, scarlet suede
still in the box, smelling like sex

pomegranates, the seeds plumped open
their dark juice seeping into the butcher block

whole cherries in preserves, full
in your mouth, a thick spoonful,

fat raspberries, autumn apples, the memory
of a rich cabernet or spicy shiraz,

sun-warm tomatoes from your garden
thick steaks rare and soft,

their blood speaking tongues in your mouth,
your flannel nightshirt, tartan-frayed and forgiving

the dresses from your youth burning
in the closet like coals from a good fire,

salmon when they are dying,
maple leaves when they are dying,

your favorite color before you knew
any better, first color you sang,

the color you love in your mouth,
color that announced your birth into the world.

At the Keukenhof

He's dead seven months, and I'm walking through fields of tulips
on a trip planned long before he choked his last breath.
They're so bright and hopeful, it hurts to look.

Rich swaths of color sweep in front of me,
petals open to sun, bursting with a pure energy—
a passionate kind of praying.

Only flowers that bloom once a season, for just a few weeks
erupt in such concentration of color. They remind me
of his laugh. I wish I'd taken him here.
He who loved intensity over almost anything,
would have felt it in these flowers.

> See, I would have said, *tulips that look like ballerinas,*
> *fringed and frilled tulips, multi-colored parrot tulips, double peony tulips,*
> *star-shaped tulips, lacy, open petals, thick bold petals, cream-colored,*
> *butter-colored. Purpled blacks they call Queen of the Night,*
> *intense orange-petaled ones tipped with yellow, their petals sword-like,*
> *giant reds and yellows with petals so open*
> *a small animal could cradle inside.*

In the distance, fields of red tulips, so many it looks as if the ground itself is red.
They could be poppies if you squinted your eyes a bit, the only other flower that
has the penetrating color of a tulip.

As I walk, encircled by color, I think, suddenly, of Dorothy and her companions
traipsing through a field of poppies in *The Wizard of Oz*, my only other virtual
experience with such masses of flowers.

Help, help, Scarecrow and Tin Man shout. Glinda waves her wand
to make snow cover the poppies, our heroes wake up,
and the optimistic twinkle voices sing:
you're out of the woods, you're out of the dark, you're out of the night,
step into the sun step into the light—

Here in these fields, grief drifts
alongside waves of tulips,
radiant, yearning.

Prayer for a Son

May your soul now be with the creek,
may it swell and flood in spring, brimming
with excitement and wildness
as you sometimes were in this other life,

> ebbing and emptying in winter
> to reveal what had been hidden
> in those spring floods—
> the wounds and bones of your heart.

May the small fish that live here
nibble at your ashes, finding them
sweet and filling,
and may the dusts of your body fall

> like pollen on the spring wildflowers,
> deepening the pinks, yellows,
> and lavenders of their petals
> until their colors are like wells
> that lead to another way of knowing.

May the insects sense the presence
of your spirit as they make trails
through your leavings,
may summer rains join with you, and
together may you enter the thin crusts
of this soil to reach the roots of oak
and cedar, juniper and cactus.

> May you overfill their veins with that joy
> you sought but rarely found
> until you burst into acorn or berry or fruit.

And when the wind blows, may it catch
and scatter the dust of you on wing of bird
or butterfly, on fur of squirrel or rabbit,
coyote, cougar, or wild horse,
may you fly with them to strange places
those you have left behind can neither know nor imagine,

and when you are root and wing, seed
and flower, when you are bone and breath,
then may we be blessed to hear you

in song of bird and cricket, may we see
you again in the mad blinking
of the fireflies, and in the silence after
the poem's last word.

Notes & Acknowledgments

p. 37 "Facebook Post: Three Weeks Before You Die," is an edited post from Gray's Facebook, posted November 21, 2014. He rarely posted to Facebook.

p. 62 "Less a Song Than a Compilation of Beats." Gray, who recorded under the moniker "Beige," wrote of one of his compositions, "Weekend Beats Slow," that it was "less a song than a compilation of beats": "Weekend Beats Slow" (2013) https://soundcloud.com/beige-1

p. 74 Lyric excerpts from "Radio Free Europe," by Bill Berry, Peter Buck, Mike Mills, and Michael Stipe. R.E.M., 1981, Hib-Tone Records, Vinyl; "Harborcoat," *Reckoning*, by Bill Berry, Peter Buck, Mike Mills, and Michael Stipe. R.E.M., April 9, 1984 by I.R.S. Records. Produced by Mitch Easter and Don Dixon, Vinyl; "Driver 8," *Fables of the Reconstruction*, by Bill Berry, Peter Buck, Mike Mills and Michael Stipe. R.E.M., September 1985, I.R.S. Records. Vinyl.

p. 77 "Your mind aches . . ." from "Parking Lot Nights," Ghosthustler, Alan Palomo and Gray Gideon, 2007. https://www.youtube.com/watch?v=X-vaH6s8LckU

p. 79 *It's no problem of mine but it's a problem I find living a life that I can't leave behind. . .*" from "Bizarre Love Triangle," by Gillian Gilbert, Peter Hook, Stephen Morris, Bernard Sumner. *Brotherhood*, New Order, 1986. Factory Records. CD.

p. 84 "Optimistic Voices," Herbert Stothart, Harold Arlen, EY Harburg. From *the Wizard of Oz*, Metro-Goldwyn-Mayer, 1939.

~

An early version of "Letter to My Son, Winter," was published as "What I can See, Mid-Winter, in my Backyard," *In the Middle of the Middle West*, Becky Bradway, ed., Bloomington: Indiana University Press, 2003

"Three of Swords," *Kestrel*, Fall, 2009

"A Perfect Game" and "On a Trail in the Languedoc," *Saranac Review*, Fall 2011

"Crook," and an early version of "[it comes down to this]," *Pittsburgh Poetry Review*, Spring 2016

"The Grief Committee," "Suit of Swords," "Ode to Needles," and "The Good Mother" (published as "Where My Shadow Lives") *MockingHeart Review*, Spring-Summer, 2016

"First Rehab," "The Grief Committee," "[it comes down to this]," and "The Drug-Pusher Friend Speaks," *Gris-Gris: An Online Journal of Literature, Culture and the Arts*. Summer, 2016

"Versions of Heaven," *Masque & Spectacle*, September 1, 2016

"Reasons to Live: The Color Red," *Pittsburgh Post-Gazette*, May 19, 2017

"Feral," *Postcards, Poems and Prose*, 2017

2017 & 2018 Releases

Apocalypse Mix by Jane Satterfield
Winner of the 2016 Autumn House Poetry Prize, selected by David St. John

Heavy Metal by Andrew Bourelle
Winner of the 2016 Autumn House Fiction Prize, selected by William Lychack

RUN SCREAM UNBURY SAVE by Katherine McCord
Winner of the 2016 Autumn House Nonfiction Prize, selected by Michael Martone

The Moon is Almost Full by Chana Bloch

Vixen by Cherene Sherrard

The Drowning Boy's Guide to Water by Cameron Barnett
Winner of the 2017 Rising Writer Prize, selected by Ada Limón

The Small Door of Your Death by Sheryl St. Germain

Darling Nova by Melissa Cundieff
Winner of the 2017 Autumn House Poetry Prize, selected by Alberto Ríos

Carry You by Glori Simmons
Winner of the 2017 Autumn House Fiction Prize, selected by Amina Gautier

Paper Sons by Dickson Lam
Winner of the 2017 Autumn House Nonfiction Prize,
selected by Alison Hawthorne Deming

For our full catalog please visit: http://www.autumnhouse.org

Design and Production

Text and cover design: Kinsley Stocum

This book is typeset in Cheltenham, a typeface for display use designed in 1896 by architect Bertram Goodhue and Ingalls Kimball, director of the Cheltenham Press. "Owing to certain eccentricities of form," writes Daniel Berkeley Updike, "it cannot be read comfortably for any length of time." But he concludes: "It is, however, an exceedingly handsome letter for ephemeral printing."

This book was printed by McNaughton & Gunn on 55# Glatfelter Natural.

Sheryl St. Germain's poetry books include *Making Bread at Midnight, How Heavy the Breath of God, The Journals of Scheherazade*, and *Let it Be a Dark Roux: New and Selected Poems*. She has written two memoirs, *Swamp Songs: the Making of an Unruly Woman*, and *Navigating Disaster: Sixteen Essays of Love and a Poem of Despair*. She co-edited, with Margaret Whitford, *Between Song and Story: Essays for the Twenty-First Century*, and with Sarah Shotland *Words Without Walls: Writers on Violence, Addiction, and Incarceration*. She directs the MFA program in Creative Writing at Chatham University and is co-founder of the Words Without Walls program.